The Further Adventures

of the Luckiest Bastard You Ever Saw

An interview with Steven Soderbergh on the making of *Kafka*

January 18, 1992, Beverly Hills Hotel,

Beverly Hills, California

and on the telephone, February 17, 1992, from his home in Virginia.

By Nicholas Pasquariello

Port Bridge Books
San Francisco, California

Steven Soderbergh's directorial credits

(courtesy IMDB)

2013 Behind the Candelabra (TV movie)
    (Emmy award)
2013 Side Effects
2012 An Amazing Time: A Conversation About End of the Road
    (video documentary short)
2012 Magic Mike
2011 Haywire
2011 Contagion
2011 The Last Time I Saw Michael Gregg
2010 And Everything Is Going Fine (documentary)
2009 The Informant!
2009 The Girlfriend Experience
2008 Che: Part One
2008 Che: Part Two
2007 Ocean's Thirteen
2006 The Good German
2006 Building No. 7 (short)
2005/I Bubble
2004 Ocean's Twelve
2004 Eros (segment "Equilibrium")
2003 K Street (TV series)
    – Week 10 (2003)
    – Week 9 (2003)
    – Week 8 (2003)
    – Week 7 (2003)
    – Week 6 (2003)
2002 Solaris
2002 Full Frontal
2001 Ocean's Eleven
2000 Traffic (Oscar for Best Picture)
2000 Erin Brockovich
1999 The Limey

1998 Out of Sight
1996 Schizopolis (uncredited)
1996 Gray's Anatomy
1993-1995 Fallen Angels (TV series)
　　　– The Professional Man (1995)
　　　– The Quiet Room (1993)
1995 Underneath
1993 King of the Hill
1991 Kafka
1989 Sex, Lies, and Videotape
1987 Winston (short)
1985 Access All Areas (video short)
1985 Yes: 9012 Live (video documentary)

With more than thirty-four producer credits and thirty-seven director credits to his name, Steven Soderbergh has proven more of a successful Hollywood mainstream director than could have been reasonably predicted given his first two psychologically arrresting and accomplished features: *sex, lies and videotape* (1989) and *Kafka* (1991). For someone who began with virtually no experience directing actors, Soderbergh has shown himself enormously adept if not brilliant in casting and directing some of finest performances in recent decades: Julia Roberts' Oscar-winning performance in *Erin Brockovich* (2000), and Michael Douglas in *Traffic* (2000), Soderbergh's best-director Oscar.

Soderbergh's most commercially successful film was the soft-core pornographic *Magic Mike* (2012), with a ratio of about seven to one between budget ($7M) and grosses ($113M), according to *boxofficemojo.com*. The following extended nearly verbatim interview shows Soderbergh to be a surprisingly easy going, candid assessor of his own strengths and weakness as a director and, as it turns out, his own future director of photography. This Q+A portion of this interview has never been published in English before, and the second summary article at the end of this piece only in *Chaplin*, the Swedish-language magazine of the Swedish Film Institute, Ingmar Bergman's old hangout. The interview is a virtual verbatim transcript of our extended conversation in person at the Beverly Hills Hotel and over the phone from his home in Virginia. This interview might not have seen the light of day if it had not been for poet, translator, scholar and teacher Bill Zavatsky's generous and meticulous editorial assistance for which I am most grateful. The author assumes full responsiblity for the accuracy of this interview.

Q: We have an hour, right?

SS: Yeah.

Q: How's it going? Have you been doing this all morning?

SS: Not too much, for about three hours. I just had some photographer shooting me for forty minutes, so I haven't done my countdown yet.

Q: I'm not getting you at the end of many weeks of interviews, am I?

SS: Oh no. I'm actually at the first leg of what will eventually be a tour of sorts. Believe me, it's minor league compared to what I went through on *sex, lies....* That was long.

Q: How long was it?

SS: I did 350 interviews in six months. I don't think I've reached fifty yet from when we started shooting *Kafka* 'til now.

Q: How many in total do you think there will be for *Kafka*; have they [*Kafka's* publicists] told you?

SS: I've probably got another fifty or seventy-five in the States, then Europe, which is still unclear right now in terms of release pattern. I know I'll need to do some, but I don't know for how long. Last time for *sex, lies...* we did a twenty-day trip. I don't know what it will be this time.

I know we're going to open in France in March. I know that will be first because [executive producers] Paul [Rassam] and Claude [Berri] are financing the film. I don't think we've made a deal in Scandanavia yet. It may have been negotiated, but I don't think it's been struck.

It wasn't until recently that Paul had a composite print that he could show 'cause we were using all of the ones that we had.

Q: How many were there?

SS: Initially there were only four and it wasn't until about ten days ago that the run of release prints started. We're also doing the prints at Duart in New

York at my insistence and they're not accustomed to dealing with high volume and they don't make very many prints very quickly.

He [Paul Rassam, executive producer of *Kafka*] just recently got his hands on one, so he's just now starting to screen it for people who he made deals with who hadn't seen the film, and now he's starting to show it to people in territories where there are no deals.

Q: Was Duart the lab you used for *sex, lies...* ?

SS: No, but they are the ranking black and white laboratory in the States.

It's more the norm when you're doing volume to go to a larger lab or a lab where you can get a better deal to just kind of crank out these prints. But in this case it wasn't smart.

We'd done the internegative and the interpositive and release prints of *sex, lies...*, and we had some really nice-looking prints. When Miramax came on they asked if we could do the release prints at a lab that they use. We said fine. They never looked as good as the ones we saw that came out of CFI [aka Consolidated Film Industries].

But mostly because it [*Kafka*] was black and white, we said they have to be done at Duart, because at least I know what we'll be getting.

Q: Did you do a test at Duart or was it Walt's [Lloyd, *Kafka* cinematographer] choice?

SS: Walt talked to all of the labs that deal with black and white. Clearly Duart deals with it more than anybody else. Because we've had some trouble in printing when we were shooting.... The prints were light, and Rank in London was never as consistent as we wanted them to be. As soon as Walt started to talk to Duart he was in synch with them.

It's a very temperamental stock, and the printer lights are completely different than color in terms of increment. I think there are five lights to a stop, in theory. That was the problem at Rank. We'd ask for a twenty-six instead of a twenty-five, and it would come back a stop different and we couldn't figure out why it was happening.

Q: So that the difference between the twenty-six and twenty-five settings was not gradual.

SS: No, not at all, and it should be. And it turns out that the temperature of the bath can exert an abnormal amount of influence over the printing. Duart was aware of that and very on top of it and was willing to run special baths for us.

Q: Where do all of the prints so far released come from?

SS: They all come from Duart.

Q: Did you see the *Variety* review?

SS: Yes.

Q: There was actually some criticism of the quality of the release print.

SS: What can I say? I think he was wrong. I disagree.

Q: It's a very subjective judgement.

SS: Yeah, it is, but "washed out" is a term that I think I could prove in a court of law is not accurate. If you want to say there are too many grays, especially the print that I know that he saw, which was a camera negative print that Walt and I had seen personally that looked pretty tasty. Anyway, that's Todd's [McCarthy, *Variety* film reviewer] privilege.

Q: What first attracted you to Lem Dobbs' script in 1985?

SS: Strangely enough, the potential accessibility of it. That is not a word that I would have ever applied to Kafka or any of his works. The fact that it was exciting....I had read some Kafka and liked it, but had never thought of his life or a straight adaptation of his works as being very cinematic.

Kafka's work - somewhat movie resisitant

I think that he or his work are somewhat movie-resistant. So Lem, I thought, had successfully avoided those mine fields and come up with something that was exciting.

Q: What do think makes *Kafka* somewhat resistant to filming?

SS: Because his stories, if they climax at all, tend to climax on an idea level and never an event level. They never climax in a way that an audience *en masse* would find satisfying. They also tend to be somewhat repetitive, especially *The Trial.* As much as I like it, I find it somewhat repetitive. And Welles adaption [*The Trial,* 1963] of it had faults inherent in the material. It's a good adaptation of that piece but that piece, is not necessarily movie material.

It's funny, the things the movie has so far been taken to task for are the very things that drew me to it: the murder/mystery, the kind of pulp adventure aspects of it are what I found really engaging because it's a mystery/thriller with a fascinating subtext. It's been in some cases those very elements that have irritated some critics.

I've been stunned at the proprietary attitude that some critics have taken toward this icon. It just strikes me as strange.

Q: Meaning no one should make any films about Kafka....

SS: There's that, tinged with They certainly shouldn't make this one. That surprised me, coming from an American I found it kind of presumptuous. Whereas in Europe, where the film is just being seen by journalists and distributors, they're so relieved that it's not a chore to sit through. They have no trouble with the idea that it's a fantasy. They get it.

That was weird. I expected mixed reviews. I didn't expect people to completely disregard the kind of what-if. I don't know. Does E. L. Doctorow come into this kind of heat when he writes one of his books that kind of fabricates reality. I don't think so.

The New York and LA reviews during the initial run were very mixed. In the case of Kenneth Turan he aimed an out and out slam at the conceit at the heart of the film.

Influence of *The Third Man*

Q: Why is *The Third Man* one of your favorite films?

SS: It's a film about disillusion, which I'm attracted to, and which certainly *Kafka* and *sex, lies and videotape* have in common; in the case of *The Third Man* (1949, Carol Reed) because there's an American at the center of it. It's about a specific kind of disillusion and a specific kind of naivete that I relate to very strongly. I feel like Holly Martins [Joseph Cotton in *The Third Man*]. I can just as easily put myself in that situation, certainly as somebody growing up who didn't step outside of this country until I was 21. It [*The Third Man*] exerted a certain fascination because of the evocation of postwar Vienna. Part of the thrill of going to Prague was having a first-hand experience. Prague is almost like a living *Back to the Future* tour. It just exists in an undiluted form as it must have existed centuries ago. And so that had an appeal.

Then anybody who is interested in making films has to be drawn to the imagery in a movie [like *The Third Man*] which is so powerful. It was an imagery that we really didn't want to copy directly. You pay a debt to that because you can't shoot a movie in black and white at night in East Europe and not pay a debt to it.

Q: Excuse me, you say you wanted to copy it?

SS: No, we didn't want to in any direct sense. At the same time you can't avoid it, you are making a genre film and you cannot...I was so disoriented by *The Shining* [1980, Stanley Kubrick,], which seemed to me to be an anti-genre film. It was a horror movie with no shadows. When I saw it, it struck me as odd, and I had no desire to turn my back on the genre and *The Third Man* is the top of that genre.

I think it's a better film than *Kafka*. I watch it constantly.

Q: At what point did you decide—is "model" the right word?—to use it as a model for *Kafka*?

SS: No, I think reference is a better word.

Q: When you read the script, did it immediately occur to you that *Kafka* would have it antecedents in *The Third Man* ?

SS: Oh, yeah. Although I read Lem's [Dobbs, *Kafka*'s screenwriter] first draft which had 30 to 35 pages of biographical material that I immediately cut out when we began to move forward on the film five years later.

Q: You don't mean dialogue?

SS: No, scenes with his family, scenes with his father, lengthy scenes with his fiancée. All things that for me pulled away from the mystery of the film. The film kind of walks a line as it is between Is it Kafka? Is it not Kafka? And this [biographical material] tipped it too far...there was too much that was really real about him, and yet it still had that weird third act. And I felt like these things are diverging to too great a degree for me. I want to stick to the mystery thriller, get it further away from Franz Kafka as a real person and go with that.

Q: So it was originally too much of a biography or biopic.

SS: Well, yeah, part of it. That was the weird thing. A third of it was, and then there was still this mystery-thriller-horror film even grafted onto that. I wanted to make it a lot leaner.

Irony in *sex, lies and videotape*

Q: There were some reports that the early drafts of *sex, lies*...did not have as much humor as the later drafts.

SS: Yeah, that's probably true, and I still think the film doesn't have as much humor as it should.

Q: What difference would it make?

SS: It needed another level of irony. I think Graham's [James Spader] problem is taken a little too seriously. If I could have had three more months I would have had that distance and it just would have been a little funnier. It would have had more of a sense of irony about it.

Q: How might you have done that?

SS: I don't know because the film's strengths and faults are the speed under which it was made, the fact that it happened very quickly. There is a certain fervor about the film that is the result of it happening fast, and maybe I would have lost that. So you live with it.

Even the difference between those first drafts and what eventually was a fourth draft, that distance was more apparent with each draft and it got a little more funny. The best example of it right now in the film is Graham saying "I look around me and I see John and Cynthia and you, and I feel comparatively normal." Which is such a crazy statement. It's such an absurd statement for him to make, and is one of the biggest laughs in the movie because clearly he's really screwed up. The picture needed more of that, more of a sense that he really doesn't know that his problem at some level is interesting, and then finally is just funny because he's so out of it.

It just needed more of that.

Q: If Graham is screwed up, the wife that he ends up with at the end is screwed up as well.

SS: I think they all are. And it's funny, somebody was taking me to task not too long ago about the good characters and the bad characters in the movie; the promiscuous sister is seen as the bad character. Why was that? That wasn't my feeling at all. They all were troubled to me, and I didn't make that distinction and still don't.

Making that film was a very precious and comfortable set of circumstances: small crew, my home town. Part of the design about doing *Kafka* was to do the opposite, to do something that I didn't know if I could do and go somewhere that I knew would not be comfortable and just kind of confront that.

Q: How did your expectations compare to the reality of the shoot?

SS: It was hard. It was difficult. I don't think it was difficult like *Bridge Over the River Quai* (1957, David Lean).

The Hardest part of making *Kafka*

Q: What was the hardest part of it?

SS: The hardest part of it was keeping the film in my head. They're still scenes in the film where I was clearly treading water and I didn't have my hand wrapped around the central feeling of the film. And that has to do with rhythm, the pitch of the performances, where the camera is, and then there are some scenes where I know I was right on top of it. So I feel like I found the film late, later than I would have liked.

Q: How could it have been otherwise?

SS: I can only assume that if I had been more rigorous in the development process that I would have found the film sooner.

Q: Rigorous in what way?

SS: I don't know. But it is somewhat distressing to me that the film came to me so late, that it jelled for me so late. It's a strange thing, you make a film over the course of 10 or 12 weeks; if you move off compass two degrees every day, when a month goes by you're somewhere else from where you started. It can be a very subtle and gradual process of losing the central idea of the movie. And I just think that happened in a couple of cases.

We reshot almost 20% of the film this past spring [1991]. By that time I really had the movie in mind, and all of that material is exactly what I wanted it to be.

Q: This is in Prague?

SS: Some in Prague and some small sets that were reconstructed in London that we had previously built in Prague.

Q: What did you reshoot?

SS: A little bit of everything. Everything in the Castle that doesn't take place in the microscope room was reshot; the hallways, Murnau's office. Anything in which you don't see the microscope or the lense room was reshot mostly because I didn't like what happened. I didn't like the way it looked. We weren't able to exert the control over the corridors that we would have liked, so we ended up building those in London so we could get that pools-of-light look.

In some of the scenes between Theresa and Jeremy I had tried to force a relationship between the two of them that the structure of the film couldn't support; so I reshot some of those scenes. And then little things here and there. A couple of transitional things.

Not the literal end of the film but the post-Castle pre-office sequence was all reshot. The scene with the inspector in the morgue at the end was a new scene. The death of Gabriella was reconceptualized in the reshooting and handled much differently than it was in the first version of the film. In the first version of the film he meets her in the Castle. She is standing in an endless line waiting for God-knows-what, obviously drugged. He can't even have a conversation with her. Through circumstance he's drawn away from her and she's whisked into some other room. He later confronts her on the bridge after he'd left the Castle, where it's clear she has been released in order to kill him. She isn't able to do that, and throws herself off the bridge.

It was a very kind of *Wuthering Heights* (1939, William Wyler) ending, which is great if you're making *Wuthering Heights* but we weren't, and I felt it was wrong. So we came up with a way of dealing with her in the Castle, where they just miss each other. She is later found and Kafka is brought to her in the morgue and we know that it wasn't a suicide. Although a lot of people have asked why does he comply, why does he say yes? Is it a suicide?

And I felt that it was a very ambiguous response that he makes, because clearly she knows enough and he knows enough to feel that their pursuits were eventually going to end like this; and that it was suicidal behavior as far as he was concerned.

Q: Could you be more specific as to where the overall problems with the production originated.

SS: No, I think it's strictly my approach. I'll give you an example. Kafka has just followed Burgel [Joel Grey] into the bathroom, thinking he has Eduard's [Vladimir Gut] file or he has some information in this package that will help him figure out what happened to Eduard. As it turns out Burgel just has some period pornography and he's just going into there to relax.

Kafka comes back and in the next shot we see him at his desk, the bell rings, people are going home. Burgel comes and says you've got some extra work, you have to stay late. That shot takes a minute and a half for all those things to happen. I was insistent in doing it in one take. It's not very vital information. There isn't an emotional core to that little scene. Why I chose to belabor it like that is an example of me looking at it and going: what was I thinking? The film should be moving here. Why am I being so languid? The time to be languid is in the following scene where he is working at night and something happens and you want to slow the film down because it's about to explode. It just should have been dispensed with. Instead I'm lingering.

As a result I asked Cliff Martinez, please write some music to cover this because it's dragging, I have no cutaway. I shot it like this. I'm stuck. There are a couple of scenes like that where I didn't provide myself with an out. As my own editor I have nobody to blame but myself.

Q: How could you have done it differently?

SS: I could have staged it in a series of shots that enabled me to compress those events. We're halfway into the film at that point, almost exactly an hour into the picture. As you know, things are about to start moving a little more quickly. It's just a very simple indication of my placing this idea of doing it in one [take] above the needs of the film, and that was a mistake.

I ended up doing two cutaways there. Jeremy originally goes through this whole speech while sitting there, which seemed endless when you watched it on screen.

Q: What was your intent?

SS: My intent was to slow the film down because the bomb's about to go off. Again, though, there's a way to give a sense of boredom without boring people.

Q: What is the difference?

SS: The difference is portraying a character as being bored as opposed to boring the audience. I think there I was boring the audience.

Q: How could you have shown him being bored without boring the audience?

And I should have allowed myself more options by staging it in a way that I could have accelerated the pace in editing, and I should have accelerated the rhythm of the scene in the dialogue. Because there are lines that I like but there are also lines that are making statements, and you're always asking for trouble when they're delivered in a serious tone.

Q: When did you realize you found the movie?

SS: Halfway through the shoot, even though that microscope stuff occurred late in the shoot, I finally found the rhythm....[Other scenes that exemplifies this are] the two scenes with the assistant after they turn sinister. (A) They turn up at Kafka's apartment and (B) they are taking him down these steps and along this wall and then Bizzlebek [Jeroen Krabbé] hits them both over the head. Those scenes have exactly the rhythm that I wanted almost the whole film to have, almost Howard Hawks kind of pace.

All of the reshot material had that feel: the scene in Eduard's apartment where she [Gabriela, played by Theresa Russell] is gathering things and trying to get out of there. One of my favorite scenes where he runs into the anarchists in the alley after coming out of the café; when he says that Gabriela's disappeared. [They respond] Yeah, we know. It's happening so fast that it's funny in a way. That was the way I wanted the whole film to be, and it doesn't have it; parts of it do. I just found it too late in some cases.

And because I don't like to shoot a lot of coverage, I didn't have the option, in a lot of cases, of accelerating the movie in the editing.

Q: You might have been able to save it if you had done more coverage?

SS: Yeah, but that's the style of the movie that I wanted [which] didn't allow for that. In general I don't like to shot a lot of coverage and I usually don't. In many cases I was asking for things that made Walt's [Lloyd, *Kafka*'s cinematographer] job a lot harder, 'cause I tend to ask for complicated masters that stop and start and move into closeups and move out of closeups.

It would have been a lot easier [for him] for me to chop it up into his shot, her shot, stepping out of frame, cut, go into a frame. That makes his job easier to cut. There were scenes in the office, for instance, where at one point, especially when you're in Kafka's cubicle after he gets promoted, where I was encompassing almost 210 degree views of the set with three glass partitions around us, moving in and out of closeups. That makes Walt's job very hard because not only does he have to deal with lighting the whole set, he's also got to deal with reflections. It was a shot that started low with a 21 [mm. lens] and then came up to above eye level, so there was no place to hide. I would ask for that stuff on a regular basis.

Q: This is in one continuous shot?

SS: Yeah. That makes Walt's job really hard. And at the same time we're all going, Come on, let's go!

It would have been easier for me to chop that scene up. As it turns out I like the way that particular shot played.

You're also in the situation where the whole take has to be perfect, and when you're talking about a 2 1/2 or 3 minute scene, it takes a while.

One of the scenes in the reshoot in Eduard's apartment with Theresa [Russell] and Jeremy [Irons], we were up in 18 and 19 takes; just again and again and again because there was a lot of movement. You've got to be here by the time he gets there, and I wanted the whole thing to play very fast.

Working with actors

I'll digress very briefly. I met [director and writer David] Cronenberg last week for the first time. We'd spoken, and I asked him about acting in *Nightbreed* [1990] and whether or not that illuminated the actor's plight for him. He said "Yeah, I actually at one point found myself about to say: you mean you want me to walk and talk at the same time?" Because, he said, it's really hard. I never realized it, I was so focussed on just saying something that the concept of moving was a new one. He said it was really interesting, and that the loss of control on the part of an actor...that he was completely at the mercy in many cases of somebody who was doing it much differently than he would have. He said it was really interesting.

I'd love to be on the other side.

Q: You have never done any acting?

SS: Nothing except for the high school play.

Q: One of the strengths of your films is seen in the casting and in the fine performances you get out of your actors.

Where did you learn how to work with actors; how to choose the right ones for the right parts?

Q: What do you say to actors when you're directing them?

SS: As little as possible if I can. I read a piece in which I was described as an actor's director. The writer had watched me work with an actor and written, here's the paradox, he doesn't say very much, and it's very low key, and there doesn't seem to be very much exciting give and take. What that person missed was that by the time I reach the set my work with the actor has essentially already been done. It's done in rehearsal and in the time I've spent with them getting to know them. We've joked around, we've had beers or whatever. I've gotten a sense of them, they've gotten a sense of me.

Every actor requires a different director in a way. They all need to be dealt with differently. Some need access to you, some don't. Some want to talk about the work, some want to talk about anything but the work. So by the time I get to the set it is just now about the work, and my comments tend to be: [you are projecting] too small, too big, you're exhibiting an awareness of certain events that you shouldn't have yet. I just want to guide them. I hate telling them what to do 'cause I find that tedious. I could never give an actor a line reading.

Q: In connection with the making of *Kafka* Jeremy Irons said in an interview that in order to be the director you have to be the father and that the actor has to be a child in the hands of a father-director.

Did you play that role with him?

SS: It's just hard for me to imagine myself as Jeremy's father as it's probably hard for you to imagine me as his father. I think I know what he means. I think the worst possible situation for an actor would be to feel nothing for his director. I think it's important to have either an intense like or dislike for your director. But to be directed by somebody who is a non-entity, I imagine, would be a nightmare, just as it would be to have a parent who is just a cypher and not a human being.

I think in that regard you are looking toward your director as this central figure in this film existence you have for ten hours a day, the authority figure. To have something to play with or play against I imagine is really important.

Q: Is it fair to say that you never felt you were playing the father role to Jeremy's child role?

SS: No, mostly because he doesn't behave like a child and mostly because I felt like, and it's my goal to make it feel this way, that it was a real collaboration.

Certainly Jeremy knows or at least trusts that I have the film in my head and that I will consider each idea and make a decision about whether or not it fits in that film, that I have final word in that regard. But my attitude toward running a set is pretty egalitarian. Ideas come from the second assistant cameraman as often as they do anyone. It's pretty wide open.

Q: I'm fascinated by the idea that at a certain point you found yourself connected to the working vision of the film.

When did that happen on *sex, lies....*?

SS: That one I had from the beginning because I had created it. I knew it was there because it was something very personal. And unlike *Kafka* it wasn't a movie that was trying to mesh a lot of different elements. *Sex, lies...* to me was a movie that grew out of some personal things, but also an appreciation of films like *Five Easy Pieces*, *The Last Picture Show* and *Carnal Knowledge,* and the kind of adult dramas of the early seventies. So I knew what I was going for. Whereas *Kafka*, although it had roots in German Expressionism, Carol Reed, and Fritz Lang, it was a movie that was trying to spin a lot of plates on sticks. I felt that at certain times I let a couple of them fall.

Q: You're making it sound as if a lot of this was out of your control; that the point at which it came together was intuitive or mystical.

I just started to go yeah, okay, now I know

SS: Yeah, out of my control in the sense that the question of whether or not I could have brought about my cohesion of that vision in a calculated way, I don't know, 'cause it certainly didn't all of a sudden happen. I just started to go yeah, okay, now I know.

Q: But you've lived with this script for years, haven't you?

SS: Not in the intensive way that happens in pre-production and production.

Q: How much time was spent in pre-production planning?

SS: About 12 weeks then 10 weeks of shooting plus two weeks of reshooting.

Q: Did you rewrite the script with Dobbs?

SS: A bit. I supervised his draft. Then, when we got to Prague, I did some rewriting on my own, all of which was jettisoned when we reshot and the reshoots were primarily written by Lem [Dobbs].

Q: Are you saying that you think initially the script had the voice, then it lost it and got it back?

SS: No, it had the voice. It lost it in the scenes that I had rewritten, and then regained it when those scenes were reshot.

Q: You've been quoted as saying that the part of the filmmaking process you enjoy most is the editing.

Why is that?

SS: Because you're sculpting now. You've spent however many years essentially constructing the stone and now you're carving the figure. It's where all the elements come together. It's where you begin to see the movie.

Q: What if the elements are not there?

SS: Then you go back and reshoot, 'cause sometimes they aren't.

Q: Even now, after you've been able to go back and reshoot, you're not entirely satisfied.

SS: I essentially did all the reshooting that I could morally justify.

Q: And budgetarily too?

SS: With the film as it exists now the things that I would change would involve going back and constructing Kafka's office again at Barrandov

Studios [Prague]. I couldn't really do that. It was huge. That set was built as part of a $1 1/2 million deal in a flat deal that included crew. That whole set is gone. And at a certain point you're dealing with diminishing returns. The things that I would change are not things that would suddenly make the film work, assuming it didn't work. I fixed those things.

It was horrifying when we went back to Prague to reshoot. I saw a location right next to the Castle that I'd never been shown before that I would have staged a major sequence in had I seen it. I saw it the last night we were in Prague in May; I'm looking at Walt and going, Why didn't we see this?

The budget versus reshooting

Instead of the quarry area, where the guy gets stabbed and Kafka slips down the hill, I would have staged the sequence there. It was this incredible eerie piece of land with trees that looked like drooping skeletons on sticks, at the foot of the Castle with a high wall, and it was exactly what you wanted for that sequence. It was really creepy. And nobody's ever shown us this place before. It was perfectly accessible. I couldn't at that point tell [executive producer] Paul Rassam, Could I have another $250,000 to come back here and shoot this sequence?

Q: That seems like a very small proportion of the budget, though.

SS: Not at that point, when we were in the reshoots. I think the original budget for the film was $10 1/2 million, and it was clear that all in we were going to be nosing $12 million. And there wasn't anything particularly wrong with the quarry sequence. It was okay. It's just that this one would have been spectacular.

We just had to chalk it up. Curse your location guy. Nothing to do.

Q: Is it your sense that *Kafka* will get the same sort of release as *sex, lies...*got in Europe?

SS: Ultimately, yeah. It will be harder. It will take longer. I think we'll do well in Europe; which is fine. I'm certainly not commercially xenophobic. I like the idea of the film playing outside the U.S. and having a response [there].

Apparently the Japanese distributors, which is one of the few deals that we had made ahead ahead of time, were very excited. They feel it's going to do really well in Japan. And they want me to cover there and I think I will. I didn't have a chance to go there on *sex, lies...*, and it's the same distributor, Nippon Herald. I want to find out why they think it will do well in Japan. I have no concept of what the Japanese audience is like. You see the grosses, but I want to sit in a movie theater and listen.

If you're at a loss when you're watching a scene, you're not sure where it's going and somebody asks you: What are we doing, and you don't know, you can't fool Jeremy. You just have to say I don't know.

Rethinking a scene with actors during production

Q: What happens then?

SS: You sit down and you talk about it. You rip it apart and start from scratch. It happened a lot on *sex, lies....* We would stop everything, send everybody away, and the actors and I would sit down and start from the beginning in a sense, and in some cases rewrite.

It's good that everything feel like it's moving in a direction. I agree with John Ford that when you hit the fork in the road, you make a choice and you follow it. There's nothing a film crew hates more than indecisiveness and a sense of inertia. At the same time you have to cop to when you're at a loss, and it's not working and you're not sure why.

Q: And it's not always in the script.

SS: No. Usually what happens is that somehow the text has come up short in terms of providing everyone with a goal within a specific scene, and so after people bumping around for a few minutes, you begin to realize why they're bumping around.

I love editing but I love that whole process, too. It's fun.

The musical score for *Kafka*

Q: I heard a resemblance between the cimbalom and the zither in *The Third Man*.

SS: Oh, sure. Like *The Third Man* I wanted a single lead instrument that evoked a place and a time. I didn't want it to be the zither. I had a very Carol Reed-like experience. I was in a restaurant in Prague and I heard this instrument and I thought, that's the sound, that's what this place sounds like to me. Cliff [Martinez, composer on *Kafka*] visited the set, heard the instrument, went back to L.A. and tracked one down, sampled it digitally, and eventually learned how to play it on an electronic drum kit, live, which was quite a thing to watch. In his tiny apartment he could play on his electronic drum pad.

Q: A keyboard?

SS: No, with drumsticks! Since he's a drummer by nature it was ironically the perfect instrument for him to play. He essentially performs the score live on the cimbalom. So it's kind of neat.

I think he wrote a great score.

Q: I've been reading this fascinating journal you've kept, which is not mentioned much in the articles about, well, about either *sex, lives...* or *Kafka.*

The unpublished production journal

Did you keep a journal like that for *Kafka?*

SS: Well, yeah, sort of, but you know, it was strictly for my own reference. I didn't really want to to do a book like that anymore. You know, *sex, lies...* was a kind of strange set of circumstances. And Harper & R ... well, somebody had approached me about doing something like that, and I had the notes together, so I said fine. It was kind of a one-shot deal.

Q: You do have notes like that for this picture, too?

SS: Yeah.

Q: Was there a problem with the candor of it?

SS: I certainly don't think I could have, on this movie, kept the same level of candor that I had established for that book. And so, that was part of it. I just felt if you can't do it right, then just don't do it. It's a different set of circumstances, [a] bigger set of circumstances, more people and more difficulties. There are conflicts you have in the course of making a film that are just par for the course, and to lay them out in a book, I didn't think, in this case would make everybody really happy. It wouldn't serve much point but more than that for me to do another book would have been *The Further Adventures of the Luckiest Bastard You Ever Saw*. And I didn't think it would have been real interesting.

Q: Do you still feel like The Luckiest Bastard You Ever Saw?

SS: Yeah, a lot of times. *Sex, lies...*in a sense did almost come out of nowhere, so part of the fun was that whole process of the film emerging. In this case it's a lot different.

Q: Are you adapting *King of the Hill* to direct it?

SS: Yes.

Q: What do you like most about the novel?

SS: It's kind of a film about resilience, the resilience of a child who's kind of on the verse of being an adult, and in many ways is forced to be an adult before he should really have to be. I'm attracted to that. I'm really not interested in movies about teenagers [but] twelve is an interesting age to me; you're on the verge of leaving childhood behind and beginning the process of growing up and understanding what the world is really like. In this book [*King of the Hill*] this twelve year-old child goes through a series of circumstances in a pretty compressed period of time that kind of forces him to confront the world. How he deals with it I thought was pretty fascinating. So hopefully, I may have said before, if it turns out well it's something akin to *The 400 Blows* [1959, Francois Truffaut]. If it doesn't turn out well it's kind of a low-rent John Hughes movie.

Q: I read a little bit of it and it struck me that it had a fairly mature tone. I didn't read enough of it to realize what it's about. I didn't realize it's about a twelve year-old. For a twelve year-old it reads like it's [being written by] a fairly mature person.

SS: It is written somewhat from clearly looking back on something as an adult although...and that is part of the trick right now. There's a very specific voice in the writing that isn't quite a twelve year-old although the twelve year-old does emerge with a voice of his own. I'm trying to keep that without resorting to any sort of narration and it's tricky. It's not going to be easy. I think narration from a young protagonist, especially one who's not very literate can be fascinating. Terrance Malick used that twice to excellent effect in *Badlands* [1973] and *Days of Heaven* [1978] and I considered doing that but I thought no he's almost too smart to be a narrator. There wouldn't be enough counterpoint. There wouldn't be enough irony in the narration so I decided at this point not to use any narration.

Q: Will there be two points of view?

SS: No. No, I don't think so.

The voice in *Kafka*

Q: We were discussing the voice in *Kafka*. I'm not sure I understood what you meant by voice. Could you define that?

SS: I think it's two things. The first is technical. It's the structure in the speech patterns, the structure in the sentences, the choice of words. As I found out the hard way, it was very specific and very idiosyncratic and Lem [Dobbs, screenwriter on *Kafka*] and I didn't. And the second has to do with the destruction, [and] rhythm of the scene itself. I was going to say it's not normal but it's good drama in the sense that it's laid out indirectly. So when we put the first version of the film together and it was obvious to me that the scenes I'd tinkered with were the worst scenes and I asked Lem to be involved in the rewrites and he agreed...

Q: What do you mean worst scenes?

SS: The scenes in the movie that didn't work were the ones that I had played with.

Q: How did you decide that a scene wasn't working?

SS: The movie would be kind of humming along and the world that we were trying to create seemed to be intact and suddenly the scene would come on in which people spoke in a way that people spoke and behaved in a way that seemed out of kilter with that world. I knew it was because the rhythms were wrong and the speech patterns were wrong. There were other things that were wrong as well and the reshooting that was done was not just a different version of the same scene. We reconceptualized a lot of stuff, things that were wrong whether I had tinkered with the dialog or not. So it was a combination of things. And fortunately Lem agreed to work on the rewrite.

Q: Should you have been able to see this before you began shooting?

SS: What the problems that went beyond the dialogue?

Q: I'm still a little bit confused. You've got what you say are language problems?

SS: Yeah.

Q: And even that's not clear to me, what that means. What Lem had originally written was in some ways deficient in certain scenes.

SS: No. Obviously in the scenes I tinkered with I felt that I wasn't making changes arbitrarily I felt there were some improvements to be made, however making them myself I think was the wrong decision.

Q: How did you decide that there were improvements to be made?

SS: Most of them, not all of them, centered around the relationship between Kafka and Gabriella, which I was never quite satisfied with because I didn't quite know what it was supposed to be. Was it supposed to be a romance and if so that seemed a little odd since her lover and his best friend had just died and I wasn't quite sure that something should start up. Or was it just unrequited, was it just Kafka just mooning over her, which was a possibility. So I was trying to determine what is going on here. And in the initial version of a couple of the scenes between Kafka and Gabriella I tried to edge toward some sort of romantic interest and when I put the film together it seemed to be that that was a mistake. It just wasn't necessary. It was a diversion and at the very least on her part there should be no interest in him whatsoever or even interest in encouraging him to have contact with her beyond business dealings, which is really what she wants from him is some help in some business level.

Relationships between the characters

So a lot of it was pushing that relationship back to one that was more straightforward. And a lot of it was inside the Castle. What happened inside the Castle. [That]...was changed. I didn't like what happened. I didn't like the way it looked.

Q: Do you see any connection between the problems of Kakfa relating to Gabriella and Graham relating to Anne [in *sex, lies...*]?

SS: I don't think so because if only because Gabriella is a much more focussed and driven character who is on a path. Her attitude is I'm going down this road and either you walk with me or I have no use for you. I guess the difference would be more in that she is a different character and a much more driven person. I think Kafka in the movie shares certain characteristics with Graham, very basic ones, just a basic inability to understand or divine the motives of other people. Other people are just a mystery to him. And sometimes his own actions are a mystery to him.

Q: I'm still not as clear as I'd like to be about what you mean by the idiosyncratic characteristics of the language.

SS: Let me see if I can think of a specific interchange between Kakfa and Gabriella. The scene where she's clearing out the apartment is one that we reshot entirely...and it used to be...it was awful.

In the first version the scene culminated in a shouting match in which she accuses Kafka of being afraid to deal with the possibility that Eduard was murdered because it would acknowledge the fact that life is chaos and uncontrollable and unpredictable and that he wants order; and that he's trying to fit the world into this little box. And she doesn't think it works that way.

Q: I'm not sure that's clear in the movie. Do you think that's clear in the movie?

SS: No, but let's put it this way, the way in which it was laid out in this scene was too blunt. That scene had too much of a contemporary feel to it, the back and forth of it. It was too direct. And the choice of words [was] not anachronistic but didn't seem in keeping with this world. The best way I can explain it is that Inspector Grubach is a perfect example of the weird speech patterns that I'm talking about. He has a very unusual way of speaking and that was the kind of thing I'm talking about.

And Armand really understood it. It's a kind of European—especially to that area of Europe. Lem is really steeped in that, and I'm really not.

So I just didn't know how specific that voice really was until I tried to go and tinker with it. So Lem did the rewrites, and when we actually did go to London to reshoot, he wasn't able to go with us, fearing the same sort of thing arising where I might need to make changes on the spot, we brought over a writer named Howard Rodman to kind of keep an eye on things, and he did some touch up work, and ended up writing one new scene.

Q: Okay, now I'm still a little bit unclear. You say there were some problems with some scenes that you had to reshoot. That suggests you went and rewrote certain scenes which were deficient in the original that Lem produced?

Rewriting during production

SS: No, no. While we were shooting principal photography, I was tinkering with scenes. When we put the first cut of the film together, amongst the problems I had were the scenes that I had tinkered with. So, at that point, preparing for a reshoot, I asked Lem to work on some rewrites for the reshoot. While we were shooting, I had been tinkering.

Q: So you had taken his original and found some reason to rewrite it, and the result of what you rewrote was not satisfactory, so you asked Lem to come back and rewrite what you rewrote?

SS: Yes.

Q: But that suggests that there was something deficient in his original script in those scenes that you wanted to rewrite.

SS: In some cases, yeah, as I said, my intent was always to improve what was there. I obviously felt something, there were many scenes that were not touched at all. But there were some scenes where I felt like, Gee, we're not quite there, let me take a shot at this. And later, the scenes that Lem rewrote for the reshoot were different, and I think better than they had ever been on paper.

Q: So in your rewriting of those scenes, did you clarify for yourself some of those problems which helped Lem to go to another stage of a rewrite, to clarify it closer to what you were groping for, what you were seeking?

SS: Yeah, I think in a clumsy way it was a neccessary step to get to where we ended up, but it was a clumsy way.

Q: Now we were talking about the actors, too, and you were saying you would discuss with actors the goals that you wanted them to reach. Could you give me some examples of those goals?

SS: Did I use the word "goals"?

Q: I believe you did. You don't like that word?

SS: Nah, it just reminds me of when you buy your little address book calendars, and there's a little page that says "goals" on it. The only thing that leaps to mind in terms of a goal, when doing a scene, was with the assistants. The goal was always for a way for a fight to start. I just remember that as a very specific task. (Which we managed to solve...). But in terms of Jeremy, certainly, I think it was a tough role for Jeremy, deceptively difficult, because there wasn't a lot of overt motion, or what most people would consider acting.

Comparing *Kafka* to Orson Welles *The Trial*

Part of the problem I had with the first version of *The Trial* [1963, Orson Welles] was that Anthony Perkins started off in such a state of hysteria that there was really nowhere to go, and I wanted Jeremy to be able to have a place to go through the course of the film, in terms of feeling out of control. And that's tough to do. The tendency, when you don't have that much to deal with, is to do too much. Especially when you're shooting out of sequence. It's hard to keep tabs on where you should be.

Q: I wonder if one of the similarities between Graham and Kafka is... I'm thinking of one of the more fascinating aspects of your journal, the seemingly small item of the back story for Graham. I think you'd said that Spader had invented he'd had a previous marriage, and a retarded child, and he'd abandoned the child, and later you decided that was silly. I didn't ever get to the end of your journal, and I don't think you ever explained why you thought that was silly. But, both *Kafka* and Graham are very withdrawn individuals.

Why did you think that back-story was silly?

SS: Because it was! I think we could've proved that in a court of law!

Q: It's not evident to me....

SS: It was just silly because.... What I often hate in a movie is just kind of a naked attempt to explain somebody's abnormal behavior.

Q: Isn't there any explanation for abnormal behavior?

SS: There is, but I don't know if there are explanations that can be successfully compressed into the time frame of a film. I think you're almost better off leaving it to the imagination because a personality is the result of such a long series of events and experiences that, in this case, it just seems to me, what can I say? Some people are just born with a certain feeling, some sort of distance from other people. I guess that's what drew me to these two characters.

Q: You think it's genetic?

SS: I don't know. I can only say that I have always felt that way.

Q: You have felt that it was genetic?

SS: I don't know. Maybe that's a Swedish thing, maybe we'll find out. Maybe somebody'll write in when they read this interview.

Q: Is that your ancestry?

SS: Yeah, my grandfather was born in Stockholm.

Q: That's not very far back.

SS: No, not at all. He was an odd guy. He left, he was in his late teens and he had three brothers, I think. I say I think because once he left he never had any contact with his family there, and he never told us about them; we don't know who they are, or what they're doing. He completely cut himself off. From what I understand that was not unusual for an immigrant to do, but it was so severe that it makes you wonder. So I have relatives walking around over there, and I'd love to find out who they are.

Q: You haven't tried?

SS: Well, I was in Stockholm for 18 hours at one point, but I didn't have enough time. I wouldn't imagine it'd be too hard, I have his birth information and all that stuff.

Q: No. I shouldn't think it would be difficult at all.

So you didn't invent any back-story for *Kafka*?

SS: No. I mean, there's no explanation beyond what was there in his life, which is he seemed to be inherently rather a sensitive soul who grew up beneath a a very domineering father-figure. So he was just a rather nervous fellow. For me to go into the specifics beyond that would just be kind of pointless.

Q: What's your favorite anecdote about the making of this film?

SS: I've told this before. It's an Alec [Guiness] story. We're shooting in the chief clerk's office, which is fairly cramped, and we're getting set up, and we're ready, and so the assistant director says, "Okay, we're ready for Jeremy." And everybody starts looking around for Jeremy, calling his name. Where is he? Is he in his trailer? No, he's not in his trailer. Where's Jeremy? And after about 3 minutes of this, finally Jeremy, looks up from 6 feet away, where he's doing a crossword puzzle (he's a real crossword freak) says, "Oh, here I am!" And Alec looks over and says, "Ahhh, now that's charisma for you!" It was just...Alec is so funny, and catty, and everybody just broke up. He was just amazing.

Q: That is pretty funny.

SS: It was funny because in person Jeremy is rather charismatic. He's very tall, and has this amazing voice, and you notice when he walks into the room. At the same time, he works very hard at having something to focus on outside of the work. To keep himself from going crazy while he waits. To me it kind of summed up everything about this very charismatic guy, focussed so intently, and curled up in a ball in the corner so that none of us could find him.

Q: Had those two ever worked together before?

SS: No, they hadn't, and the funny thing is, they've worked together since. On an *American Playhouse-Tales From Hollywood* that Christopher Hampton wrote, that I can't wait to see. Should be very interesting.

Q: You were supposed to do a picture next called *The Last Ship*. What happened to that?

SS: I pretty much just abandoned it. It was a novel about a naval destroyer that survives a nuclear holocaust. I loved the book, I loved the subject matter, and how author handled it. The book is told out of sequence, and when I straightened it out, certain kinds of plot difficulties became very apparent, most of which had to do with the third act. I wasn't terribly pleased with the way the book ended. I think it worked wonderfully for the book. It wouldn't work for a movie.

Q: Why one, not the other?

SS: I think it worked in the book because I think the writing pulled it off.

Q: The style, the flow of the language?

SS: Yeah, and for a movie I just didn't feel it worked. Basically what happened was: they go to this island, and it's a mixed crew. And I had devised a different way to come up with a mixed crew. In the book it was set in the very near future. There it's a mixed crew on this naval destroyer, which there

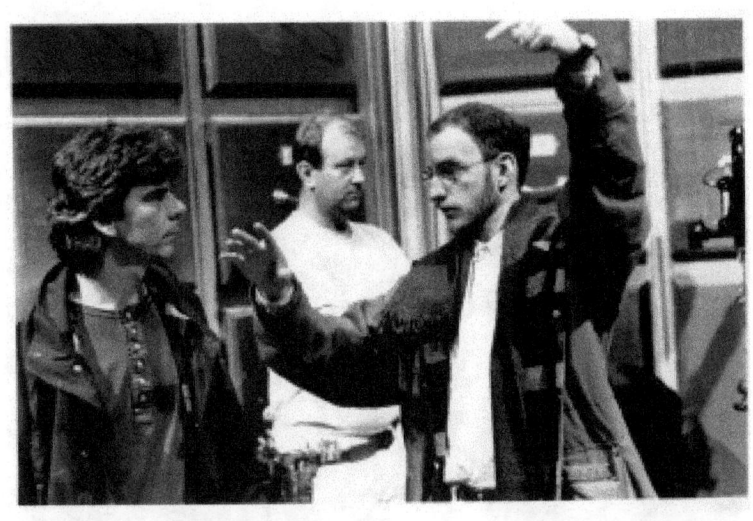

Steven Soderbergh with Director of Photography Walt Lloyd
A Miramax Films Release copyright © 1991
Pricel © 1991

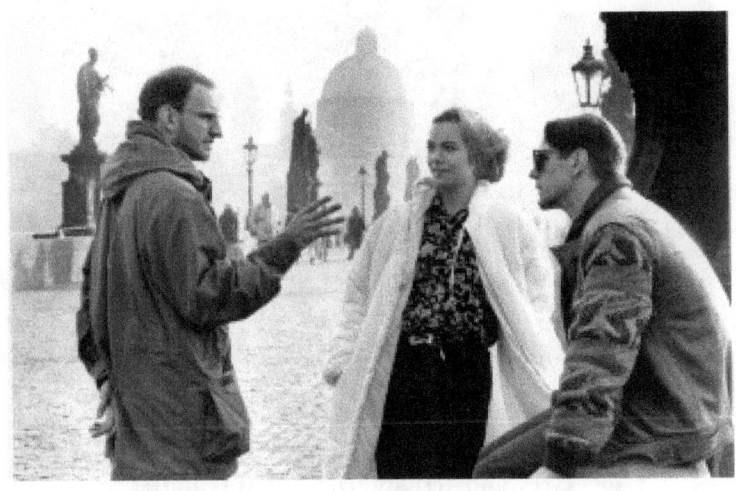

**Steven Soderbergh with actors Theresa Russell and Jeremy Irons
shooting in Prague, Czechoslovakia**

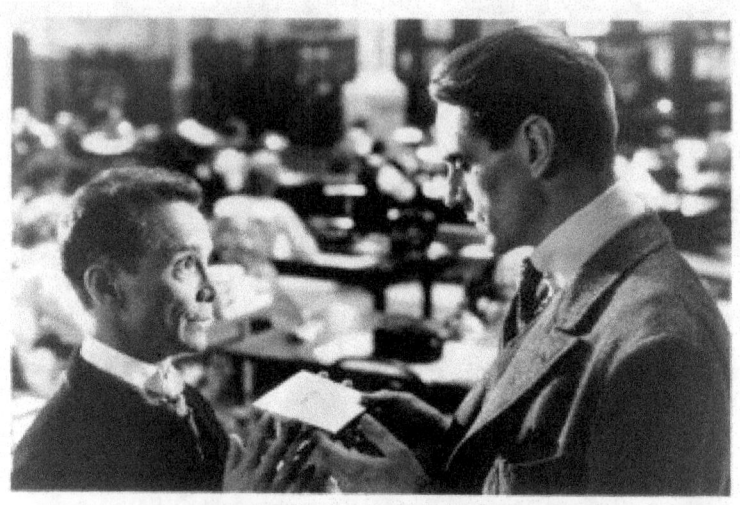

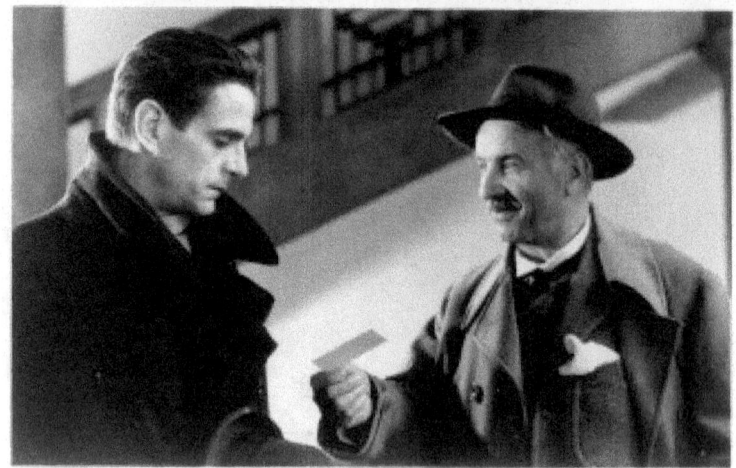

**Joel Grey and Jeremy Irons (above) and
Jeremy Irons and Armin Mueller-Stahl (below)**
A Miramax Films Release copyright © 1991
Pricel © 1991

isn't right now, and I devised a different way, a way I was real happy with, to get women on this boat.

When they hit the island, they come up with this kind of rotating plan of everybody getting together, and monogamy is outlawed. The leader of the men and the leader of the women have this illicit affair. The long and the short of it is, they are eventually forced to leave the island because of the insane actions of one of the sailors, and they go to the South Pole, where they find an abandoned military base. At this point they're hooked up with a Russian submarine, and everything seems to be okay and they plan a voyage in the Russian sub to see what actually happened to the rest of the world. Basically this guy and this woman get off free. Having had this affair, they kind of stop it, and nobody knew about it!

I had a real desire to have them have the affair, but to be found out and stripped of their power by the rest of the people [and forced] off the island. I thought, Oh, great, that's interesting! Unfortunately, it also put me in the position of at some point having to redeem the captain, and I didn't know how to do that. I just got stuck. Then, obviously, world events kind of made this film less relevant.

Q: The new world order.

SS: Yeah, it was really inconsiderate, I thought.

N: (*Laughter*) How about *The Leather* script?

SS: *Leatherheads*, which is a tentative title.

Q: And where does that stand?

SS: Well, we made an offer to an actor who I'd had in mind from the very beginning of the script, and as of last month he was unable to commit yet. Basically he said: if I have to answer now, I have to say no, because I can't say yes. And I said, well if I go and do *King of the Hill* next, and leave *Leatherheads* open, as kind of a standing offer, will that increase my chances of you saying yes? And he said yes. Well, that's what I'm gonna do because I really want him to do it.

Q: You can't say who this is?

SS: Not yet.

Q: When can you? When he accepts, definitely.

SS: We kind of caught him at a bad time. He was doing two movies back to back, and when we needed his answer he was on one of his four days off between the two movies. I don't think he was in the mind to sit down and commit to a movie where he runs around in the rain and mud a lot. This summer, when things have cooled out a bit and he's less busy, I think that'll be a better time.

Q: Is he American?

SS: Yeah.

Q: What is the origin of the script?

SS: The script was written by my brother-in-law and his writing partner. They both work work for *Sports Illustrated*. I'd heard about this idea kind of secondhand from my wife while I was in Prague, because my brother-in-law and his partner were pitching this idea to Paramount, who'd professed interest in a football movie. However, when Paramount found out it was a period piece, they immediately rejected it, and went for what eventually became *Necessary Roughness*.

SS: This is late October or November of '90. When I come back from Prague, and I'm editing the first version of *Kafka*, and attempting to revive *The Last Ship*, without much success, I called Duncan, my brother-in-law and said, "What happened to the football project?" "Well, y'know, it got turned down, so we're just kinda sitting on it." I said, "Well, look, I'm gonna call Universal and Sydney Pollack, and Al Blaugh, who is also involved with *The Last Ship*, and see if I can swap the football movie for *The Last Ship*, keep all the same people, but just switch the material, because I think this is a great idea. I haven't seen this movie yet and I think it's a great idea.

So that's what we did, and I basically just supervised the writing of the script.

Q: Were you working on *The Last Ship* script alone?

SS: Yeah.

Q: You've worked on scripts alone, you've done some collaborating, as on *Kafka*, your original script on *sex, lies...*and you did a rewrite with Lem, and now you're adapting a novel. Could you compare the creative challenges of these three different ways of working?

SS: Well, there's so many different kinds of writing, period. One of them is just sitting down of your own accord and writing something new, that nobody has asked you to do, and that you haven't told anybody about.

Q: Spec.

SS: That is the most fun because of the total freedom of it, including the total freedom to abandon it without anybody ever knowing that you even attempted it. That's great. Then there's writing-for-hire, writing something "original" for hire, which I attempted to do once, and it was actually I think I talked about it in the journal. It was gonna be a kind of spy movie for *Outlaw*, that I abandoned because-*sex,lies...*dropped on my head, and I started writing that. So I never even completed that, so I can't even say what that would be like. Working with somebody, believe it or not, based on the experiences on *Kafka*, I really liked a lot. I really liked working with Lem because he's extremely bright, and there's a healthy sort of running debate going. Ideas aren't strictly accepted and implemented. Somebody brings something up and the other person plays devil's advocate. It's just fun, and he and I have talked about doing something else together, from scratch. Adapting the novel...I'm very curious to see how *King of The Hill* is going to turn out.

Q: Is this the first time you've adapted a novel?

SS: Well, the first time since *The Last Ship.*

Q: Which you didn't finish.

SS: Oh, I finished it. There's a draft, I handed it in.

Q: But you're not happy with it.

SS: No.

Q: You wouldn't shoot it.

SS: I wasn't happy with the last act. I was happy with a lot of the other stuff. I was pleased with how I was able to compress a 616-page novel into a 125-page script that I thought was a pretty good compression of that book. And I was pleased with the integration of things I'd invented into things that were straight out of the novel. I mean, despite the fact that I didn't want to make it into a movie because I thought it had third act trouble, I thought it was a decent job of adapting a very difficult book.

King of the Hill is gonna be much more difficult, because it has...the conflicts aren't quite as overt, and that's always a problem in making a movie.

Q: How do you prevent yourself from letting it slip?

SS: I think you have to prevent yourself from being cynical.

Q: Ha! I'm laughing because I think that's probably the most prevalent problem in Hollywood, and in moviemaking, and probably masks the whole encyclopaedia of wrongs and ills and misunderstandings about what filmmaking is. I take it that one of the ways you do this is by living in Virginia.

SS: It helps, I think. It's funny, I just read a script last week that I had a response to that I haven't had in long time, in the sense that I read a script that somebody else wrote, that I immediately said: I want to make this movie. It was sent to me by Mark Johnson, of Baltimore pictures, who I'd worked with on *Kafka*.

And he said, "Great, can I have the writer call you, because he'd love to hear that?" And I talked to the writer, and I said, "I don't understand. Why has this script been around? This is an amazing script. Why isn't somebody making this movie?" He said, "I hate to say it, but I don't think you're very in touch with Hollywood. This script just doesn't, by Hollywood standards, have the kind of requisite elements that they consider important for a "hit" movie.

"There is no romance, there is no character that is the good guy or the bad guy, there's a lot of ambiguity." He says, "You have no idea how important that stuff is to studio people."

So maybe my distance from it gives me a slightly different point of view. But, God, if it means I respond to material like this, which was just wonderful, then great.

Q: Do you read scripts?

SS: Occasionally. It depends. In this case I knew the subject matter, and I was kind of predisposed to being interested. And that's usually what happens; normally my agent'll call and say "Read this, read that," and I'll say, "Look, I'm booked for a while, let's keep it shut." But occasionally I'll get a call from somebody that I know, like Mark, who says, "I've got this script about such-and-such. Would you like to take a look?" Again, if the subject matter is something I'm interested in, or I know the writer, or it's based on a book that I like very much, then I'll take a look.

Q: The conventional way that Hollywood directors work is that the script has to come through a producer or an agent. It's fairly rigid. Do I hear you saying that that's not the way you are currently operating?

SS: No, that seems to be it. I mean I do get these through my agent or through a producer through my agent. It seems to be going that way, although I do see things ....I have a friend of mine, that I went to high school with in Baton Rouge, who's a filmmaker, and graduated from the California Institute for the Arts. He wrote a script a couple of months ago that I thought was really good, that he sent to me, and I'm trying to help him get that set up. And I've encouraged him, because he's a friend of mine.

[I said to him] when you've got it done, send it to me, I'll see what I can do. I reserve that sort of open door for people who are old friends of mine. In this case I hope it'll result in something I'll be involved with, even in just a sort of consigliere position getting the film set up.

Q: One of the last things we talked about, just as I was leaving the Beverly Hills Hotel, was editing. That you had said you had edited *sex, lies, and videotape* on a rudimentary system; and then the [*sex, lies and videotape*] journal mentions that it was edited on a videotape. And *Kafka* was edited on the EditDroid [originally developed by LucasFilm]....I worked a little while for Lucas on the manual for that machine.

SS: Oh really. There wasn't even a manual when I started. At least not one that could really be called a manual.

Q: No, I don't think they ever finished the manual.

SS: When I was out there in the summer tweaking the final version of the film, there was this huge thing on somebody's desk, and I said, Is that the manual? [And they said] we're still working on it. The problems I had with the machine invariably had nothing to do with the manual.

Q: What problems did you have with the machine?

SS: Whenever I'd have a problem, it was because a bit of software was acting up, and I needed to reset something, or whatever. They gave me some very basic information from one of their classes, you could take at the time. And then the person who had taught me this machine had kind of drawn up their own little 10-page thing by hand, about the most basic things you'd be using a lot, and that turned out to be fine. It's tough because the little documentation that I had was not really laid out the way I think an editor would lay it out. But, I love the system.

Q: When I used it a few years ago...

SS: Before they shut it down and revamped it?

Q: Yeah.

SS: Oh, it was a mess! I would never have used it back then!

Q: They had these 1/2 hour platters....

SS: That's still the case.

Q: I think that goes to the heart of something fundamental in the videodisc technology.

SS: I don't think that's a problem.

Q: No?

SS: Because the access time is still so fast, I never found that to be a problem. The problems with the way they initially envisioned the machine were many and significant, and they completely revamped the whole system. It works really well, now. I'm really glad they did. It took a lot of gumption on somebody's part to...they shut down for two years and started from scratch almost, and boy, they really did it. I've already talked to them about *King of the Hill*. I'm really hooked.

Q: So you saw the system before it was revamped?

SS:...My boss had gone to NAB, (I was working at a video production house at the time) and he brought back the brochures and a tape. We sat down and looked at it, and said, this is a nightmare! The way the software is working is needlessly complicated and nobody who's ever touched a piece of film would want to play with this!

Q: What kind of system did you edit *sex*...on?

SS: It was a Sony RM-440, which is the basic Sony editor. The most basic Sony editor.

Q: That's even more basic than the CMX, isn't it?

SS: Oh God, yes. but the funny thing is, it's a great little machine, and I had no trouble. It just meant that I had to manually log the whole show. It was tedious.

Q: Lastly, here, you spoke of being disappointed in not being able to use a location that seemed so crucial to the downhill racing scene. How did you find locations for *Kafka*? Did you hire a Czech location manager?

SS: We had a gaggle of Czech location scouts, and art directors. They really did take us everywhere but that one location. It was just a fluke. It was an easily accessible and very public place on the other side of the Castle. It was just happenstance that we never got to it. The problems the film has, and it has it's flaws, and I forgive it its' flaws, have nothing to do with that scene. It just would've been incredibly striking....

Q: And the reason you didn't hire a location manager for *sex..* was because that's where you're from and you've spent so much time in that town? What are you most proud of about *Kafka*?

SS: I think, I was really pleased with the kind of world that was created, within the context of the film. I thought it was an interesting, detailed world, away ultimately pleased with the sense of time and place within the film.

What follows is the original article entitled ,"Kafka meets the man from

Baton Rouge", based largely on the above interview as it appeared in

Chaplin magazine in Swedish in 1992.

In 1989 Steven Soderbergh created a stir in the film world when he became at 26 the youngest director to win the Palme d'Or (Grand Prize) at the Cannes Film Festival. His independently produced feature *sex, lies and videotape*, his first, made for just over $1 million, has since earned over $100 million worldwide [The $100M figure was wildly quoted in early 1990s media reports; in 2014 boxofficemojo.com reports a world-wide gross of $36M]. *Sex...* also had the happy fate of receiving widespread critical praise. Soderbergh is the audacious sort of artist who rarely achieves success in commercial American cinema; he had written *sex, lies...* in a way that Jack Kerouac might applaud, out of the white heat of inspiration, mostly on the road driving from his native Baton Rouge, Louisiana to Los Angeles, California. The director points out that both the film's strengths and its weaknesses derive from the speed with which it was made.

Arguably the most famous young director in the world, for his second picture Soderbergh had the pick of numerous commercial Hollywood projects. He choose the rather non-commercial *Kafka*, a pseudo-biographical *film noir* thriller written five years before by an unconventional Hollywood writer, Lem Dobbs. What most appealed to the director about the script was the murder mystery pulp adventure that forms its central plot, and the theme of a disillusioned central character—so reminiscent of *sex*.... Steven

Soderbergh also found Dobbs's script surprisingly accessible considering it was based on usually inscrutable Kafka material. (Ironically in the U.S. media many critics ridiculed *Kafka* for the very reasons that drew Soderbergh to the story).

The director was aware that there were some risks involved in venturing into the unchartered waters of what was for him a completely new film form; so different in its psychology and *mise-en-scene* from *sex*.... These risks may or may not have been worth taking. They surely affected the quality of the completed film of *Kafka*.

In electing to make *Kafka* Soderbergh readily acknowledged the influence of one of his favorite films, Carol Reed's masterful thriller *The Third Man*. Like the film's American central character Holly Martins, Soderbergh had rarely travelled abroad. When Soderbergh went to Prague in 1990 he said he felt like his naive compatriot Holly Martins (Joseph Cotton) must have felt, thrust into war-torn Vienna in search of his elusive buddy Harry Lime (Orson Welles).

Clearly the artistic heights Reed had reached in creating the ambience of a time, place and mood also inspired Soderbergh to make *Kafka* in Prague, which for him evoked feelings of post-war Vienna. Says the director exuberantly, "Prague is almost like a living *Back to the Future* tour, it just exists in an undiluted form as it must have existed centuries ago."

Similarly the powerful black and white imagery of *The Third Man* had its effect. "It was an imagery that we really didn't want to copy directly ...[but]... you can't shoot a movie in black and white at night in East Europe and not pay a debt to it," the director notes. (Except for a vaguely surreal color climax all of *Kafka* was photographed in black and white).

A creative tension existed in Dobbs's original script between noir-thriller and biographical story elements that still haunts the film. Soderbergh saw as the driving force of the story the mystery the central character almost inadvertently gets involved in. Since one third of the script started off being about Franz Kafka's real life relationships with his father, fiancé and family, Soderbergh found it necessary to virtually—but not entirely—write Franz out of the film. "There was too much that was really real about him and yet it still had that weird [*noir*] third act. I wanted to stick to the mystery thriller, get it further away from him as a real person and go with that," he comments. (Jeremy Irons' character is always addressed as Kafka, never Franz or even Mr. Kafka.)

The Kafka that remained, though based on Franz Kafka's life, was one the director defined vaguely as "inherently a rather sensitive soul, who grew up beneath a very domineering father-figure...a rather nervous fellow."

Kafka's plot revolves around the disappearance of petty bureaucrat Eduard Raban (Vladimir Gut), who as Kafka's best friend and office mate may have been involved in revolutionary anarchist activity in 1919, a very gray year in this fictional Czech place. Kafka becomes involved in the search with Raban's lover, Gabriela, making him an accomplice after the fact.

In relation to the driven character of Gabriela, who sees life as chaotic and unpredictable, the director says Kafka is someone who demands that there be order in the world. In one intense scene shot but edited from the final cut, Gabriela accuses Kafka of being afraid to deal with the possibility that Eduard was murdered, because for Kafka to do so would acknowledge how uncontrollable the world is.

When asked to compare Graham, the videographer from *sex...*, with Kafka Soderbergh concedes they may share some affinities. Both, he says, are withdrawn individuals who possess "an inability to understand, to divine the motives of other people." To both other people are a mystery.

Comparisons between *Kafka* and *sex, lies ...* are inevitable, if not always salutary. Soderbergh says *sex, lies...* was made under "a very precious and comfortable set of circumstances—small crew, [and in] my home town. Part of the design of *Kafka* was to do the opposite—to do something that I didn't know if I could do and go somewhere that I knew would not be comfortable and just kind of confront that."

Whereas *Kafka* was Lem Dobbs' original script, Steven had written *sex...* out of the angst of his own life. It could hardly have been more personal. As he later interpreted the film, it had all of the elements of a confessional, complete with admissions of guilt and a commitment to lead a new and better life.

"Unlike *Kafka* it wasn't a movie that was trying to mesh a lot of different elements. *sex, lies...* to me was a movie that grew out of some personal things, but also from an appreciation for films like *Five Easy Pieces*, *The Last Picture Show* and *Carnal Knowledge,* and the kind of adult dramas of the early seventies. So I knew what I was going for, whereas *Kafka*, although it had roots in German Expressionism, Carol Reed and Fritz Lang, was a movie that was trying to spin a lot of plates on sticks. I felt that at certain times I let a couple of them fall."

For Soderbergh the primary dilemma he faced in making *Kafka* had to do with his connection to the vision of the film, or as he puts it, "keeping the film in my head."

"There are still scenes in the film where I was clearly treading water and didn't have my hand wrapped around the central feeling of the film. And that has to do with rhythm, the pitch of the performances, where the camera is. And then there are some scenes where I know I was right on top of it. So I feel like I found the film later than I would have liked."

Here it is hard not to interject some comment, not to say appreciation of Steven Soderbergh's unusual and forthright candor in discussing his work. As the old saying goes, he is his own worst critic. He is quite simply one of the most candid directors working in big time cinema with the likes of actors Jeremy Irons, Theresa Russell, Joel Grey, Alec Guinness, Armin Mueller-Stahl, and producers Mark Johnson, Stuart Cornfeld (partners with Barry Levinson in Baltimore Pictures), and Paul Rassam (Claude Berri's partner). All of whom worked on *Kafka*.

It is the mark of an accomplished director that he is willing to take responsibility for his work in a total sense. This rarely happens especially when there are production problems.

Clearly Soderbergh is happier with scenes he was able to reshoot about halfway into his 10-week shooting schedule, by which time he said he found his working vision of the film. These scenes often have the frenetic pace of the best work of screwball comedy director Howard Hawks *Bringing Up Baby* (1938), and *His Girl Friday* (1940), are among Soderbergh's favorites and are mirroed in the antics of *Kafka*'s two assistants whose machine-gun-like non-sequiturs ricochet around their cramped office.

The following are among Soderbergh's favorite scenes.

Kafka's absurdist assistants show up at his apartment, drag him away down steps, and along a stone wall. His friend, the stonecutter Bizzlebek emerges out of the shadows and hits the assistants over the head, allowing Kafka to escape.

Kafka emerges from a crowded, smoky café saying to the first people he meets: Gabriela has disappeared. The anonymous faces respond: yeah, we know.

In retrospect, the director suggests that his style of shooting the film with little coverage—cutaways, alternate camera angles—allowed his editor few options in post production. (Soderbergh is his own editor).

He illustrates some of the complexity of his shooting method.

"In many cases I was asking for things that made [Director of Photography, Lloyd] Walt's job a lot harder, 'cause I tend to ask for complicated masters that stop and start and move into close-ups and move out of close-ups. It would have been a lot easier [for him] for me to chop it up into his shot, her shot, stepping out of frame, cut, go into a frame.

"There were scenes in Kafka's cubicle after he gets promoted where I was encompassing almost 210 degree views of the set with three glass partitions around us, moving in and out of close-ups. That makes Walt's job very hard because not only does he have to deal with lighting the whole set, he's also got to deal with reflections. It was a shot that started low with a [wide angle] 21 [mm. lens], and then came up to above eye level, so there was no place to hide—in one continuous shot.

"It's also difficult because the whole take has to be perfect, and when you're talking about a 2 1/2 or 3 minute scene, it takes a while [to get it right]. For one of the scenes in the reshoot in Eduard's apartment with Theresa and Jeremy, we were up in 18 or 19 takes, because there was a lot of movement—you've got to be here by the time he gets there, and I wanted the whole thing to play very fast."

Curiously one of Steven Soderbergh's strengths as a director is his keen eye and ear for acting talent. This was evident in the dead-on casting to type of *sex, lies...*, which was equally effective in *Kafka*. You probably never would have guessed that Soderbergh's never taken an acting class nor done any acting.

Where does this natural gift come from?

"I've always liked actors. That's half of it—I take them seriously and I want to hear their ideas and I treat their input with respect. At a gut level I always felt that a comfortable actor is a good actor: an actor who is unafraid of doing something wrong or doing something silly is going to be somebody who is going to try things that they wouldn't normally try. And that an inhibited actor—unless you're making a film about an inhibited character — is never going to deliver completely.

"In a sense I don't have the language even to talk to them. I've never taken an acting class."

What then does he say when directing performers?

"As little as possible, if I can. By the time I reach the set my work with the actor has essentially already been done. It's done in rehearsal and in the time I've spent with them getting to know them. We've joked around, we've had beers or whatever. I've gotten a sense of them, they've gotten a sense of me.

"Every actor requires a different director in a way. They all need to be dealt with differently: some need access to you, some don't. Some want to talk about the work, some want to talk about anything but the work. So by the time I get to the set my comments tend to be: [you are projecting] too small, too big, you're exhibiting an awareness of certain events that you shouldn't have yet. I just want to guide them. I hate telling them what to do 'cause I find that tedious. I could never give an actor a line reading."

He believes the Kafka role was a deceptively difficult one for Oscar winner Jeremy Irons "There wasn't a lot of overt motion, or what most people would consider 'acting.' Part of the problem I had with the first version of *The Trial* [Orson Welles, 1962] was that Anthony Perkins started off in such a state of hysteria that there was really nowhere to go, and I wanted Jeremy to [emotionally] have a place to go through the course of the film."

In his published diary of the making of *sex, lies...* Soderbergh describes a back story he and James Spader wrote for Graham's character. The brief narrative of the life Graham leads before the film begins was prepared to help Spader understand his character's motivations. In a previous marriage Graham was imagined to have had a retarded child, which he later abandoned.

Before shooting started, Soderbergh decided without explanation that the backstory was silly.

Later when pressed to say why, he answered: "What I often hate in a movie is just kind of a naked attempt to explain somebody's abnormal behavior.... I don't know if there are explanations that can be successfully compressed into the time frame of a film. I think you're almost better off leaving it to the [audience's] imagination....

"Some people are just born with a certain feeling, some sort of distance from other people. I guess that's what drew me to these two characters [Graham and Kafka]."

If people are born with this feeling does that mean it's genetic?

"Maybe that's a Swedish thing."

Steven Soderbergh's grandfather emigrated from Stockholm to the States early this century. "He was an odd guy, because once he left he never had any contact with his family there, and he never told us about them. We don't know who they are or what they're doing....

So I have relatives walking around over there, and I'd love to find out who they are."

Currently Soderbergh is adapting A.E. Hotchner's coming of age novel *King of the Hill* to direct. Though he doesn't particularly enjoy books about teenage life, he was attracted to the theme of resilience at the heart of *King*. An adult in the novel reflects upon boyhood experiences, yet the boy's voice is strongly felt, hence a dilemma for the adapter of this material: how to unify both voices without using a narrator, which Soderbergh doesn't want to do.

"If it turns out well it will be something akin to [Francois Truffaut's, 1959] *400 Blows* . If it doesn't turn out well, then it will be a low-rent John Hughes [*She's Having a Baby* (1988), *Ferris Bueller's Day Off* (1986)] movie."

Steven Soderbergh turned down an offer to publish his diary of the making of *Kafka* because he thought it would have to be titled *The Further Adventures of the Luckiest Bastard You Ever Saw*.

About the author

Nicholas Pasquariello has been writing internationally about the more technical aspects of filmmaking for more than two decades for a wide variety of trade magazines and other publications including *American Cinematographer, Mix, On Location, LOCATIONS, Chaplin, Premiere, Producer Magazine, Millimeter, ACTION, Filmmakers Newsletter, the San Francisco Chronicle, Videography, Video Systems, BROADCAST*, and *USA Today*.

www.ingramcontent.com/pod-product-compliance
Lightning Source LLC
Chambersburg PA
CBHW072204170526
45158CB00004BB/1763